# Salt of the Mind

# Salt of the Mind

ALEXANDRA VILLANUEVA

Copyright © 2024 Alexandra Villanueva, All rights reserved.

No part of this publication may be reproduced, stored in a retrieval system or transmitted in any form or by any means, electronic, mechanical, photocopying, recording or otherwise, without prior permission of Halo Publishing International.

The views and opinions expressed in this book are those of the author and do not necessarily reflect the official policy or position of Halo Publishing International. Any content provided by our authors are of their opinion and are not intended to malign any religion, ethnic group, club, organization, company, individual or anyone or anything.

For permission requests, write to the publisher, addressed "Attention: Permissions Coordinator," at the address below.

Halo Publishing International
7550 WIH-10 #800, PMB 2069,
San Antonio, TX 78229

First Edition, August 2024
ISBN: 978-1-63765-621-1
Library of Congress Control Number: 2024911360

The information contained within this book is strictly for informational purposes. Unless otherwise indicated, all the names, characters, businesses, places, events and incidents in this book are either the product of the author's imagination or used in a fictitious manner. Any resemblance to actual persons, living or dead, or actual events is purely coincidental.

Halo Publishing International is a self-publishing company that publishes adult fiction and non-fiction, children's literature, self-help, spiritual, and faith-based books. We continually strive to help authors reach their publishing goals and provide many different services that help them do so. We do not publish books that are deemed to be politically, religiously, or socially disrespectful, or books that are sexually provocative, including erotica. Halo reserves the right to refuse publication of any manuscript if it is deemed not to be in line with our principles. Do you have a book idea you would like us to consider publishing? Please visit www.halopublishing.com for more information.

*For those who've never known my name
But met me in these pages*

A thief in the night
Trying to swindle my heart
Too bad
I didn't leave it out for you

I was like you once
Lost and in doubt
This world is a big place
And we have no idea what our spot is gonna be
But take a deep breath
It may find you
When you think you're the least ready.

I've come to learn that the term "family" is relative. My family is decided by more than the blood in my veins. My family is alive, and my family is beyond. My tree grows through those I put my love and faith into.

*Mi familia es más grande que cualquier límite creado por el tiempo y el espacio.*

My gospel comes from the adoration on your lips.

The first time you brought me home,
I made you take the long way.
Baby,
I would have had you drive around in
circles if it meant more time next to you.

## Salt of the Mind

I never claimed to be a church girl.

But for you, I'll always be ready to pray.

He calls me beautiful
He says I'm worth it
He reminds me every day
I hope one day
I'll believe it
Before it leaves his lips.

## Salt of the Mind

It's like a subconscious test
I don't know the outcome
Until those tears creep out
Then I realize
You've got me done for
And my secret?
I hope you never fail.

Nothing has ever felt as natural as waiting in the kitchen, seeing you walk through the front door, and hearing "I love you" fall from your lips.

Toothbrush? Check
Shampoo and conditioner? Check
Deodorant? Check
Hairbrush? Check
What else…? Oh, okay.
Babe? I left my heart at your place.

Your jacket feels like a safety vest against the world; These ghosts of your arms will always hold me tight.

I miss the grand movements between our souls, dancing together, held close to each other, just to never let one fall alone.

You went out to the big, wide world
Finally got to
Spread your wings
I'm so happy for you
But I have to say
I never expected
You'd leave me behind
My chosen sister
It's okay
I guess I just wasn't
Meant to be part of
The flock
You flew into

One day she's gonna get hurt in a way
that will make her not care
She'll stop hoping, stop worrying
There will be a time that her tears will
fall but the pain
Won't subside
It will consume her
And on that day
You must pray
Pray for her and pray for those
who have wronged her
Pray for all those who may cross her path
For she will have no mercy.

It's so insignificant
A distant memory
I was trying to
Take all your time
And I remember on that walk
You tripped on the way back
I laughed as some of your drink
Spilled to the ground
You looked up
And laughed with me
That day is so small but
It's so significant
To me.

My heart on my sleeve? No, no, no, darling

It's my entire damn wardrobe.

I wonder how bold of a line
The distinction is
Of hating you
And loving myself.

I don't like being the center of attention.
It's not fun.
Honey,
You will always be the center of my attention. And that's plenty of fun.

Seeing you at work is a vision
It shows me the you that you share with the world
It tells me the you that you save for me

I love all versions of you.

You love me
You love me not
I don't know if I'll ever see
I'm exactly what you sought.

You love me
You love me not
Is it possible for you to be
The best thing I've ever caught?

You love me
You love me not
Like the earth holds a tree
I'll wrap you in my arms without
a second thought.

No car ever meant so much to me as that blue Toyota. All I ever wanted was to see it come up the driveway.

Should you need me
I'll be where the days are long
The sun is high and bright
The place that the birds sing
and the flowers grace the land
I'll be there until further notice
So leave a message
I'll find it in a bottle as the sparkling water
Sweeps me in its arms.
To whom it may concern:
*You'll find me where life thrives.*

Only when Dionysus's nectar passes my lips
Do I find my darling girl dancing in the wind
She's beauty with the world
I'll never love her less.

You may wrap your pointe shoes
and dance for the world
But I shall wrap up my fists and bloody
them for it.

Jack could have totally fit on that door.

Although, I think the real question is:
Would you have had the strength
To pull yourself up?

You may never feel as if your work
is good enough
That's okay
You can always grow
You can always strive to be better
But no matter what
Someone will always be in awe
of the simplest thing you can do
Something is better than nothing, darling.

Roadside Bouquet

*Noun*

Definition: You saw my smile in the weeds that were on the highway shoulder.

When I call you up for a drive
It's not because I need to talk
about something
It's more
It's the air on my face and the lights on the
Highway
It's the red moon reflecting the taillight blurs
It's the bass of the song we have on
as we go 90 in a 65
I call you for a drive, so for once
Whatever life has thrown at us
for the previous seven hours
We can feel free while in the arms
of the open road.

There's a reason humans have an innate fear of heights
Only the gods were meant to witness such beauty.

Dear English teacher,
I picked the color blue not because I was
Sad
But because it's like the horizon of his eyes

Dear English teacher,
I said I was exhausted, and it wasn't meant as
An exaggeration

Dear English teacher,
The number of lines I wrote
Doesn't create a bigger message
Than the words themselves

Dear English teacher
I compared her to a lily of the valley
Not because she dropped in her beauty
But because
She was born in May

Dear English teacher,
I wrote these words for you to read them as they are
Not as what they could be

I was so immersed in your being
I forgot what the rest of the world feels like
And honestly?
It's better when I see it with you.

Ripping off a Band-Aid used to scare me
I knew it would hurt
I always took it off slowly, little by little
But these days
Pulling it off in one fell swoop
Feels a lot like a familiar I used to have
And old friend of mine
That I haven't seen in a long time
That's a good thing, but alas
I felt comfort when I took off that Band-Aid.

You know what they don't tell you?
They don't tell you that crying gets harder
How your body fights against you
That the well is full, but the drain is stuck
There is no release
They don't tell you that the more you fight
The harder it is to let go.

Body dysmorphia and dress codes are mortal enemies.
Change my mind.

You're my Hume. It's like home but better because it's got u.
(Terrible, yes, but you still smiled.)

## Salt of the Mind

I wrote a letter in school once
My best friends read it in geometry
I found out later
My words made them cry and
The teacher took my letter

I think when he must have read it
He might have seen the truth I bared

Because I wrote of a little boat
Who was doing all they could to stay afloat

To this day, I think of that little boat
And some days
I feel it yet again taking on water

I'll keep grabbing the bucket; don't worry
But you should know
The bucket only does so much.

The sun may have been bright overhead
But there was a mist in my soul that
Stephen King would have been proud of.

You may take my pride as arrogance
But I never claimed to be perfect
I may be Good
But there will always be work to be Great.

I hope you watch my life with laughter, in optimism, and with more than a bit of desire.

I love you is not like a Hello Kitty Band-Aid
It will not fix someone's pain
It took me a long time to learn that
Because while love should be one
of the best comforts
Those three words cannot be used
as a life ring
No matter how rough the tides are.

Please understand
I'm not needy
I'm afraid
My mind doesn't think you're asleep
It thinks you're in the hospital with no one
Knowing your name
I'm not prepared
I'm just afraid.

Would it truly be so much to ask for the chance to read those books again and not see our old, tragic love story?

*Healthy Dose of Death*
You said it sounded like an indie rock band
And I immediately wanted to write
the whole album for you.

Sometimes I write for myself.
Sometimes I write for everyone else.
Either way, the words on the page will mean
Something to someone.
That's all that matters.

The words I write, whether
for my heart to heal or for yours
to cherish, will reflect differently.
To each his own, but they are
treasured regardless.

My love language is touch
So touch me
Whether by loving me
Or by shoving me out of the way
to get to the shower first.
I really don't care
Both make me happy.

You don't really understand how important some boundaries are until someone runs through them with the determination of a marathon runner breaking through the ribbon.

You are my monster
You are my ghost
I try every day to expel you
The things you put me through

But you never concede
I don't know if you ever will
Maybe not while you're on this earth
I don't know if that will make me feel better

How dare I ask for death
Just so I can breathe
Without your knee on my chest…

You stood up and for a second
I worried that water would land on my head
I didn't flinch when you were across the table
But my skin crawled
With that glass in your hand
All I wanted was a meal and peace
But I think all I paid for
Was a bad experience and lunch I was
No longer hungry for.

Salt of the Mind

You earned your name for the love you
Harvested
I always believed it was stored away so safe
My sweet Reaper
I never imagined it to be stored in such a
Bad place
Only to have rot take hold
Please just know
I'll miss you in the early mornings
When the frost and dew still grasp the world.

Feeling your kisses across my skin; a feather was never so gentle.

You may think it's ridiculous, a girlish little thing. But there's this feeling when you receive a gift that's as special as that shiny little jewel. It's as if they brought you the prettiest rock they could find. And when you have that rock, you make it so that everyone knows who picked it out for you.

One of the oldest questions:
If you were in a room full of people you used to love, is there someone who would look for you?
Think about it
Is that the person whom you would *want* to come look for you?
Is that the same person whom *you* would look for?

You may not like what I write
That's okay
I do not always write for you, dear reader
I write for pieces of me, past and present
For the little girl who grew up
For the pain and pleasure we've experienced
I write to convey truths and secrets
That my heart is ready to exclaim
I don't always write to you, dear reader
I simply allow you to enter my world.

There's a picture of her
Hair pulled back, dressed nicely,
working hard
She's put together in this intricate yet simple
Design
And I yearn to be her
But while she sits there,
An imaginable ghost of
Who I wish to live as
I sit on the floor of my kitchen
Keeping all my pieces together.

Loving you sober is more delicate than loving you drunk.

I knew I was screwed when I realized home had a heartbeat.

My words may be dark
Sad
And lonely
But it's better to out them on the page
Than to keep them sheltered
Inside this body
That I'm trying to heal.

That genie better not even ask for my wishes. I have only been thinking about one that needs to be granted—you.

And the heavens have let loose their fury to the souls below.

The gods have gifted me such a blessing
But I must greedily say
There's no time allowance that they could
Offer
That I would deem enough to accept
with you.

My soul repeats its chant
This is wrong
This is wrong
Until the day I'm in your arms again
And I hear a better song
All is right
All is right.

Grief is unexpressed love?
Deary, deary…
I'll drown in my grief
No matter how long I've had you.

How do I become your flower?
How can I be the bright, colorful,
and alive thing that makes you grow too?
My love,
We can be flowers together
And we will grow the most wild
and beautiful garden.

You are my Tennessee orange
Nothing feels better than the warmth
on your hand
While watching these trees pass
I just want to be your Lady
May(be)

Feeling your arm reach out
In the middle of the night
It's the buoy I never expected
To always grasp so tight.

We sat on the edge of the road
Cramped in those leather seats
The radio silent
You didn't feel as I felt about that spot
For you it was new and a piece of the puzzle
You had that was me
Darling, you should know
Telling you all my stories of that house
Only made me want to make our own
So much more.

You said I sleep talk when I'm drunk
That scares me
Don't be alarmed
I just prefer to see you without the goggles
When I undoubtedly confess
My heart's desire
Is you.

See you in a bit
You never asked me what it meant
Or my strange timing of its repetition
But I always did
From the moment I closed my eyes
I welcomed your smile in my dreams.

The time has come
That I have the happy chance
Of telling you I'm coming home
Every     Single     Day
How did we get here?
How can we stay here forever?

I cleared out my books to make room for our hearts to sit together.

Some people may say that
The best kind of love is
The compulsive
Incoherent
Rash and burning kind
I've felt that
But I think I've decided
I disagree
The best kind of love
(In this poet's humble opinion)
Is the kind that feels
Like warm towels from the dryer
Like gentle rain on your cheeks
Like the sole of a new shoe
The best kind of love
Is the kind you feel every day
Without being driven mad.

My house is no longer my home
When I walk through my door
I see my bed, my pillows
My books, my clothes
My house holds my things
But my home holds my heart
When I walk into your arms
That's where I know
I should lay my head every night.

Your touch is eager in lust
Eyes teeming with love
I never waver by your heart
You have my everlasting trust.

Wooden petals
Plastic LEGOs
Rainbow in glass
I've gotten all the flowers before
But the ones I love most
Are the ones you and I are growing together.

Show the Devil your gold
The Reaper will smile at your diamonds
Hades shall burn your first-class ticket
Death knows no love of wealth
You will die a poor man if not only for
The courage you must have on your way.

You'll never know the sense of security
it gives me
To keep in my mind that the worst thing
you'll do when you're mad at me
Is eat my food and leave the toilet seat up.

86    Salt of the Mind

The issue is I have autumn bared in my soul and summer sticking to my skin.

I look at the stars
And think of you
Sometimes I hate it, and it burns my bones
But there's a small part
An ounce
That understands
And forgives.

Home is a feeling I reminisce in,
more than live

The sound of paws on laminate
The chirping of a bird surrounded
by crystal
A bowl of cereal handed down

My home is different now
But I am no less in love with the warmth
it provides.

You were meant to teach me love and
Passion
You were not meant to teach me anything
About preservation.

At the end of the day, he's just a
Boy
And she's just a girl
And all they want to do is hold
Hands,
Love each other forever,
And laugh about *Supernatural* episodes.

Poetry is not just sitting at a desk
It's racing home to you on the highway
It's remembering a passing joke
in Newspaper
It's the sun on my face in the dead
of winter
It's a warm hug from my mothers
*Poems are obscure and grand pieces of life
shared in nostalgic voices.*

I put up with your toothpaste stains
on the bathroom mirror.
You tolerate my hair on the shower walls.
But I leave you smiley faces
when I wipe it off.
And you leave me love letters
and call it abstract art.

You weren't all bad
There was good
In between the pain
Homemade strawberry milkshakes
Before the bruises.
I remember that sometimes.
The drive-through was packed
So you made me one
But it doesn't erase
What happened later.

Alternative #1

None of it ever happened
I went to class
I told someone how I felt
I locked the door behind me…
These things were done
and you never touched me.
Who would I be then?
I guess it doesn't matter
I am stronger and braver
than I ever knew I could be.

Alternative #2

I carried her
Every day through
We welcomed her with tears
and hope and fear
Our little bundle of joy
What a different world
But it is not what was meant
So I'll keep sending my balloons
And carry her in my heart.

Alternative #3

I listened to my father
My adviser I should have trusted
I stayed home and learned
My side was not a place for you
And in that, you never hurt me
My breaths would not be measured
by the pressure on my chest
You would not be the ghost
that haunts my sleep.

"Handle with Care"
A term written on my skin
Meant for the contents inside
Delicate and scarred
Best be careful with the package
For the special part
Is wrapped up tight
Just in case.

I promise my life will be more than the words on the page.

I love you through the August sun.
I love you through the February spring.
I love you through the May memories.

But I need to love myself first,
through everything.

Airports give me a strong sense of heartbreak
Am I leaving a part of something behind, or
Am I going where I can find it?

Take me to the dogwoods
Listen to that northern cardinal
I will think of those roads we walked
And the rain that fell
*Θα έχουμε πάντα Βιρτζίνια*

We love each other with all we've got
We're part of each other in every way
But I'll never be ready for the day
That the only place you remain
Is in our hearts.

Call me art
Tell me I'm a masterpiece
I may never truly believe you
But those soft words off your lips still sink
Into my mind
And give me a comforting embrace.

There is something about being Made
About being created and formed
as one thing
The love you have for your Creator
and the bond that can never be broken
*It's unconditional.*

To love someone
Is to let go
They say if it comes back, it's yours.
My pain screams to let you go.
But I hold every hope that we find each other again.

## About the Author

Alexandra is an artist, a student, and the author of *Whispers of Her Heart*. She loves writing and watching for life to inspire the next project.

ISBN Paperback: 978-1-63765-373-9

Like most rebel-idolizing, in-a-constant-fugue-state-of-awareness teenagers who are thrust into adult life while still holding the title Child, I survive merely off energy drinks, the air of parental disappointment, and Skittles.

## Let's Connect
Get to know Alexandra Villanueva

### Instagram:
A.V_Books

### Email:
ournostalgicvoices@gmail.com

www.ingramcontent.com/pod-product-compliance
Lightning Source LLC
Chambersburg PA
CBHW072159100426
42738CB00011BA/2476